S

J
796   GILBERT, Nancy
GIL   The Special Olympics

AR level - 6.8
Points - 1.0 DATE DUE

The
SPECIAL
OLYMPICS

Published by Creative Education, Inc.

123 South Broad Street, Mankato, MN 56001

Designed by Rita Marshall with the help of Thomas Lawton

Cover illustration by Rob Day, Lance Hidy Associates

Copyright © 1990 by Creative Education, Inc.

Photography by Allsport, Berg & Associates, D. Donne
Bryant Stock, DRK Photo, Focus on Sports, Globe
Photos, Hillstrom Stock Photo

Printed in the United States

Library of Congress Cataloging-in-Publication Data

Gilbert, Nancy.
   The Special Olympics/by Nancy Gilbert; edited by Michael E.
Goodman.
      p.   cm.—(Great moments in sports)
   Summary: A history of the Special Olympics from its founding by
Eunice Kennedy Shriver to the present, with profiles of Special
Olympians.
   ISBN 0-88682-311-0
   1. Special Olympics—Juvenile literature.   2. Athletes—Biography
—Juvenile literature.   [1. Special Olympics.   2. Athletes.]
I. Goodman, Michael E.   II. Title.   III. Series.
GV722.5.S64G55   1989   89-27083
796'.0196—dc20   CIP
                                                                              AC

The SPECIAL OLYMPICS

NANCY GILBERT

CREATIVE EDUCATION INC.

As the lone runner enters the stadium, a hush falls over the crowd of 60,000. The runner circles the stadium track proudly, holding aloft a lighted torch. It is the Special Olympics Flame of Hope. With this flame, the runner approaches the large Special Olympics' torch which will burn throughout the games.

As the torch is lit, the Parade of Athletes begins. The athletes march into the stadium, carrying the flags of the many countries they represent. Only a few years ago, many of these athletes had trouble running, swimming or even walking on their own. Now they are here to participate in Olympic events.

Together these 4700 competitors form the largest international sporting event of the year. The athletes come from all over the world. They come from Ghana and Kenya in Africa; from Japan and China in Asia; from Austria and Spain in Europe; and from Brazil and Mexico in North America. More than seventy countries in all have sent athletes to the Summer Special Olympic Games. And these people are only a few of the more than one million children and adults with mental retardation who participate in Special Olympic programs throughout the year.

A blaze of color has filled the stadium floor as the flags wave and the athletes' uniforms blend into a harmony of hues. The competitors gather around the stadium's stage and Sargent Shriver, president of Special Olympics International comes to the microphone. "The 1987 International Summer Special Olympics

are now open," he announces, as the spectators and athletes cheer. "Let the games begin!"

THE OTHER OLYMPICS

To understand the Special Olympics, you need to know a little bit about mental retardation. People with mental retardation learn more slowly than other people. People with mental retardation have difficulty learning the types of things taught in school, such as reading and drawing and math. Some find it hard to learn certain physical movements, such as jumping or balancing. They might have difficulty learning rules for games, or how to behave with other people. They often have trouble applying what they know to new situations. But people with mental retardation can learn. With the right training and with lots of loving help they can learn to read, write, and do math. They can learn the skills needed to do a job. And, as Special Olympics has proved, they can learn to compete and excel in sports.

All the athletes take part in the opening ceremonies' parade.

6

Eunice Kennedy Shriver, the sister of the late United States President John F. Kennedy, understood this fact early in her life. She had always maintained a special interest in people with mental retardation since her sister, Rosemary, had been born with mental retardation. In her efforts to fight mental retardation, she had been named director of the Joseph P. Kennedy Foundation, a foundation dedicated to the prevention and treatment of mental retardation.

Through her work, Shriver visited many of the hospitals and special homes where people with mental retardation lived.

The facilities were crowded and understaffed. The patients were in poor physical condition. She learned that very few individuals with mental retardation received any kind of physical fitness education. They did not have many opportunities to play, to run, or to enjoy recreation areas.

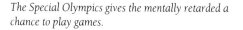

The Special Olympics gives the mentally retarded a chance to play games.

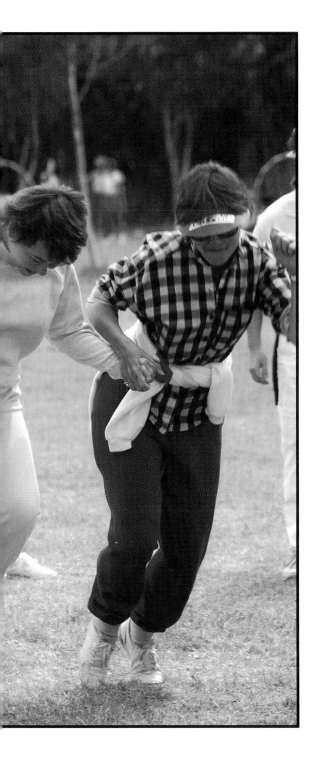

Many experts at that time thought people with mental retardation could not learn to play games or would hurt themselves in athletic activities. Eunice Kennedy Shriver felt differently.

Eunice Kennedy Shriver founded the Special Olympics in 1968.

9

In 1961 she began a summer camp in her own backyard to give the mentally retarded the opportunity to play, to run and to enjoy themselves athletically. "I decided I'd show them," she remarked. "I wanted to convince people if the mentally retarded were given a chance they could achieve."

That summer in Rockville, Maryland, 100 day campers with the help of 100 volunteers were given that chance for five weeks. The campers played volleyball and kickball. They rode horses and swam. For most of them it was the first time they had participated in sporting activities. The special attention and loving care they received from the volunteers did wonders. "I saw improvement," Shriver commented. "But most importantly, I saw them participating in things they were rightfully entitled to."

From this experience grew the idea of the Special Olympics. By 1968, the First International Special Olympic Games were held in Chicago, Illinois. One thousand people from twenty six states and Canada competed in swimming and track and field events.

Most of the athletes had never been outside their hometowns. Most had never slept overnight in a hotel. Few had ever flown in an airplane. The Special Olympians, however, took all their new experiences in stride. And at the same time, they joined with great excitement in the athletic competitions.

By the end of the Games, the athletes, their families and coaches joined hands in a giant circle of friendship and sang "Auld Lang Syne." "I thought this was a really beautiful ending," commented one coach, "to what everyone had put so much effort into, a very rewarding experience for us all."

Within a year after the first International Special Olympics Games, programs had been organized in all fifty states, the District of Columbia and Canada. Since then, as we have learned, the Special Olympics has grown even bigger. It now includes over a million athletes all over the world and hundreds of thousands of volunteers.

Any person over age eight with mental retardation may participate in Special Olympics. From the ten-year-old swimmer from Nigeria to the eighty-one-year-old bowler from North Dakota, Special Olympics is a million separate stories about a million individual people.

Nigel Pinto is a Special Olympics athlete from India who trained in track and field. He was disappointed in 1983 when he was not chosen to represent India at the International Summer Games. But he did not give up. He decided to overcome his fear of water and learn to swim. Indian Olympic swimmer Anita Sood helped him train, and in 1987 he swam for India at the International Summer Special Olympics.

Erica Levy lives in Colombia, South America. Her two sisters are world-class swimmers. Erica now wins awards too— as a Special Olympics swimmer.

Chuck Sadler has always been slow. He could not learn to tie his shoes until he was ten years old. Yet today he is a cross-country skier in the Special Olympics. His father recalls the early years when Chuck competed as a runner. "In one of the first races, a runner fell down. Chuck stopped to pick him up and helped him across the finish line."

Anyone over age eight with mental retardation may participate in the Olympics.

11

Through Special Olympics, Michelle Dumes learned to love running. Then she found out that she had a heart problem. Doctors told her she would have to give up running. Michelle insisted on having open-heart surgery because she believed it would enable her to run again. After the surgery, Michelle regained most of the strength in her heart and in 1987 competed in the International Games as a runner.

Other Special Olympic athletes have shown similar courage. There was the boy who ran using crutches. There was the girl who long-jumped with an artificial leg. There was the blind runner who followed his coach's voice around the track. A whole basketball team made up of deaf players spoke with their coach using sign language. And there was the runner who lost her race because she could not remember which way to run, but who finally found her way to the finish line and sprinted across, wearing a big smile of accomplishment. Three more Special Olympians are Michelle Sprague, Pauline Miller, and Michael Maglione.

The athletes experience a special sense of accomplishment.

MICHELLE SPRAGUE

Michelle Sprague from Texas learned to swim in her backyard pool during the summer of 1977. The next summer she began jumping off the springboard into the pool. Michelle's mother thought she saw talent in those jumps, so she took Michelle to the local YMCA for diving lessons. At the YMCA Michelle joined a class for beginning divers. "When she first started," recalled her mother, "she couldn't remember what to do from one dive to the next. But it was amazing what she could do." She soon surpassed her classmates and has been winning medals in swimming and diving competitions ever since.

Like Michelle Sprague, these swimmers show dedication to their sport.

14

Michelle's story might have been quite different. When she was a young child, Michelle's parents knew she was "slow," but no one could explain her difficult behavior. When she was eight years old doctors found that she had a condition called *Phenylketonuria*, or PKU. This condition prevents the brain from growing and developing properly. It can also cause irritable behavior.

Through a special diet, Michelle has been able to somewhat control the behavior problems. It has become easier for her to accept criticism and suggestions from her coach. Athletics has helped her use her energy productively.

Michelle's mother is the first to admit that it was just lucky for Michelle that the family home had a swimming pool in the backyard. But what began as luck was followed up by hard work, love, and determination. Michelle and her mother have driven as many as 500 miles a week to get Michelle to a practice or a meet. Michelle trains two hours each day—one hour in swimming and one hour in diving. She is a fierce competitor. "I love swimming and diving because they are my life," remarked Michelle. "And I work harder than anyone because I want to be number one. When I'm working out I think about the competition, and how I have to be ready for it."

Michelle's training and dedication have paid off. At the 1983 International Summer Special Olympic Games, Michelle was the only athlete to receive three gold medals. At the 1987 Games, she earned four. She received the gold medal in diving for which she had to complete five different dives, including a backward somersault and a backward dive with a half twist. Altogether she racked up 186.20 points—a Special Olympics world record.

The long hours of training are evident during the competition.

Special Olympics has been good for Michelle in lots of ways. It has brought her success in her chosen sports and national recognition, through newspaper and television coverage. More importantly, participating in Special Olympics has also helped Michelle in other areas of her life. "Michelle has come a long way," commented her coach. "Her patience, memory, and ability to concentrate have all improved, and she's much more consistent in her work habits. Training and competition are really the best things for her."

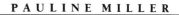

Halfway across the country from Michelle lives another outstanding Special Olympics athlete. Twenty-four-year-old Pauline Miller lives in Hampton, Virginia. In the 1987 International Summer Games she competed in the pentathlon. Pentathlon is a Greek word that means "five events." The pentathlon consists of the standing long jump, 50-meter dash, softball throw, high jump, and 400-meter run. In the 1989 Winter Games, Pauline competed as a speed skater in the 500-meter, the 800-meter, and the one-kilometer races. In the 500-meter she won the gold medal, breaking the record in the process. She earned silver medals in the 800 and one-kilometer races.

The hard work is rewarded during the medal ceremonies.

Life was not always so grand for Pauline Miller. She was born with several physical deformities that required numerous operations to correct. For many years she was withdrawn and not very sociable. Special Olympics helped open her up and boost her confidence.

Pauline attended classes for people with mental retardation until she was twenty-two. Then she spent a year in vocational training. Today, she holds a regular job as a housekeeper in the local Veterans Administration Hospital. She now lives on her own in an apartment, paid for from her own earnings. "They say handicapped people can't do anything," Pauline remarked. "I've proved to them and to me that I can do something."

The Olympics feature all types of sports, including weightlifting.

Athletes participate in the Olympics for the sheer joy of competition.

Michael Maglione first skied when he was eight years old. He has been training under his coach, Anthony Infante, ever since. Practice and hard work have helped him improve steadily as a skier.

MICHAEL MAGLIONE

"I was terrified when I saw the size of the mountain," said the skier's mother, who had never seen her son ski before. "When I got up there, at 8,200 feet in Squaw Valley and when I saw him I was so scared, I couldn't look. . . . And then I was watching him come down like it was so easy, going in and out of all the poles. It was very, very thrilling." The skier was Michael Maglione of Jersey City, New Jersey. The event was the 1989 International Winter Special Olympics in April 1989.

Like Michael Maglione, this skier enjoys the thrill of the sport.

About a year before the Fourth International Winter Games, Infante told Michael's parents that Michael might be able to attend the International Games. The Magliones had never had enough money to take a vacation, but when they heard Infante's news, they began saving so they could go with Michael to Reno if he qualified. He did qualify and, at 17, competed for the first time in an International Special Olympics. It was especially thrilling because it was the first time Michael's parents had ever seen him ski.

Maglione did well in all his skiing events. He earned two silver medals and a bronze medal in his slalom and downhill races. But Special Olympics is more than medals to Maglione. Participation has helped him grow up and become more self-confident. Special Olympics has also helped Michael in school, where he struggles with learning disabilities. He has learned to concentrate better and his memory has improved. Michael, Michelle and Pauline are just a few of the millions of individual success stories of the Special Olympics.

Coaches provide valuable training for Olympic participants.

The athletes are the reason Special Olympics exists, but many other people help to make Special Olympics possible. For example, one volunteer becomes a coach for a local gymnastics program, while another serves as a driver during a Special Olympics competition. A school club hangs up posters about an upcoming local Special Olympics meet. A scout troop raises money to buy sports equipment for Special Olympic athletes. All of these activities are crucial to the running of Special Olympics. And all of these jobs are done by volunteers.

One of the very important groups of volunteers are the coaches. There are about 100,000 Special Olympics coaches worldwide. These coaches must attend Coaches Training School to become certified in their sport or sports. They must also complete ten hours of practical work with Special Olympics athletes before being certified. The coaches' training prepares them to use the most effective techniques in working with the athletes. There is a Sports Skill Guide for each Special Olympics sport. The guides outline techniques for helping athletes improve their overall fitness, as well as competence in their chosen sport.

Some of the most visible volunteers are the "huggers." These are people who stand at the finish line of every race, or on the sidelines of other events. As each

competitor completes an event, the hugger is there to offer a hug and words of encouragement. This feature of the games helps keep the focus on the importance of participating, of trying your best.

25

Volunteers help in lots of other ways, too. They raise money to support Special Olympics programs; they make gyms or other facilities available for Special Olympics teams; they become officials or timekeepers at competitions; they donate services from their businesses.

Volunteers are so important to Special Olympics because the competition is free to its participants and to spectators who watch the events. Money raised by volunteers pays for uniforms, sports equipment, food and transportation at the Games, and printed material about Special Olympics.

Volunteers are vital to the success of the Special Olympics.

One of the people who works so hard for Special Olympics is Paula Nargi of Winthrop, Massachusetts. Nargi has a full-time job. But she also gives about twenty hours a week to Special Olympics. Nargi runs sports training programs and clinics for about 600 Special Olympics athletes and 200 coaches in the Boston area.

Nargi became involved with Special Olympics because of her brother, who has been a Special Olympics athlete for more than fifteen years. Nargi says the program has helped her brother both physically and personally. He has improved his skills and become a leader of his team.

Paula Nargi was recently named one of the outstanding volunteers in the Boston area by the United Way of Massachusetts Bay. In speaking about her involvement with Special Olympics, Nargi said, "You feel good working with these athletes because they're so appreciative. . . . My job is very challenging and it has many rewards. Working with these athletes makes everything seem worthwhile. They're all very special to me."

Besides numerous contributions by individuals such as Paula Nargi, many organizations also support Special Olympics. For example, Civitan, a volunteer service organization, was the largest contributor of money and volunteers to the 1987 Summer Games. Civitan raised $1.6 million to help the Games; additionally, more than 1,000 Civitans paid their own way to South Bend, Indiana, so they could be there to help out. Many large and small corporations have also contributed money, volunteers, entertainment, and products to Special Olympics Games.

Many children volunteer their time for the Special Olympics.

Not all volunteers are adults. Even school children help out. They hang posters to let people know about an upcoming competition. They raise money to help a Special Olympics athlete—as

little as $13.21 can buy the equipment for one competitor. They also become involved in Junior Civitan International, which has raised thousands of dollars through bike-a-thons, dance-a-thons, and Canadian snowmobile marathons.

Athletes benefit from the Special Olympics in many ways.

Being a Special Olympics volunteer can be very satisfying. Of course, it might also be a little scary at first. People with mental retardation often act "different." You might not know what to say or know how to behave. Mike Tyson, heavyweight champion of the world, felt that way before he worked with a group of Special Olympic athletes to put on a TV special in 1988. "At first I didn't understand them. I was afraid of them," he admitted. "Then I spent some time with them, and I've gotten emotionally attached to them."

OLYMPIC SPIRIT

The spirit of Special Olympics can be summed up in these words: skill, courage, sharing, joy. Like all athletes, Special Olympics athletes work hard to learn the skills they need to compete in their sports. More than that, they show the courage to work against difficult odds, to overcome handicaps that might cause many people to give up. They share their enthusiasm and successes with family, coaches, and friends. They exhibit the joy of trying, of participating, of doing the best they can.

Special Olympics helps people in many ways. New friends are made. Athletes become more physically fit and more able to accomplish sports activities. More than that, Special Olympic athletes' memories improve, they become better at following directions, and they develop a sense of responsibility. These are all skills that help them at school or at jobs.

31

Michael Maglione became more sociable, more able to join in conversations and socialize with other people. Michelle Sprague gained a new sense of responsibility; she now does chores around the house to help her parents. Pauline Miller gained the confidence to go out on her own by getting a job and her own apartment.

Not only the Special Olympic athletes benefit from Special Olympics. Their families are rewarded, too. In the past, parents of children with mental retardation might have felt ashamed or embarrassed. Today they can share the pride and joy of watching their children succeed.

Volunteers, too, benefit from Special Olympics. Their reward has been described this way: "Participation in Special Olympics quite simply, for volunteers, generates feelings of love, of connecting with the human race at the highest level."

Special Olympics is, in every way, special. It touches the emotions of all who experience it—as athletes, families, volunteers, or spectators. It teaches that people can strive for the sheer joy of it, that people can succeed by trying. In 1989, Eunice Shriver spoke to the athletes at the Opening Ceremonies of the Summer Games: "You are the stars and the world is watching you. By your presence you send a message to every village, every city, every nation. A message of hope. A message of victory.

You Special Olympians have thrilled us on the playing fields of the world. You have taught us that what matters is the courageous spirit, the generous heart. You Special Olympians are individuals we can all learn from and admire."

For more information, contact your state Special Olympics Office or
Special Olympics International
1350 New York Avenue, N.W.
Suite 500
Washington, D.C. 20005